W9-AVM-358

GRAPHIC LIBRARY™

GRAPHIC EXPEDITIONS

BUILDING THE GREAT WALL OF CHINA

AN *Isabel Soto* HISTORY ADVENTURE

by Terry Collins
illustrated by Joe Staton and Al Milgrom

Consultant:
Dr. Hanchao Lu
Professor and Director of Graduate Studies
School of History, Technology, and Society
Georgia Institute of Technology
Atlanta, Georgia

Capstone

Mankato, Minnesota

Graphic Library is published by Capstone Press,
151 Good Counsel Drive, P.O. Box 669, Mankato, Minnesota 56002.
www.capstonepub.com

Copyright © 2010 by Capstone Press, a Capstone imprint. All rights reserved.
No part of this publication may be reproduced in whole or in part, or stored in a
retrieval system, or transmitted in any form or by any means, electronic, mechanical,
photocopying, recording, or otherwise, without written permission of the publisher.
For information regarding permission, write to Capstone Press, 151 Good Counsel Drive,
P.O. Box 669, Dept. R, Mankato, Minnesota 56002.

Printed in the United States of America in Stevens Point, Wisconsin.
042010
005756R

Books published by Capstone Press are manufactured with paper
containing at least 10 percent post-consumer waste.

Library of Congress Cataloging-in-Publication Data
Collins, Terry.
    Building the Great Wall of China: an Isabel Soto history adventure / by Terry Collins;
illustrated by Joe Staton and Al Milgrom.
    p. cm. — (Graphic library. Graphic expeditions)
    Summary: "In graphic novel format, follows the adventures of Isabel Soto as
she explores the history behind the building of the Great Wall of China" — Provided
by publisher.
    Includes bibliographical references and index.
    ISBN 978-1-4296-3411-3 (library binding)
    ISBN 978-1-4296-3890-6 (softcover)
    1. Great Wall of China (China) — History — Comic books, strips, etc. — Juvenile
literature. 2. Graphic novels. I. Staton, Joe, ill. II. Milgrom, Al, ill. III. Title. IV. Series.
DS793.G67C65 2010
951 — dc22   2009001171

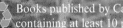

Designer
Alison Thiele

Cover Artist
Tod G. Smith

Colorist
Krista Ward

Media Researcher
Wanda Winch

Editor
Christopher L. Harbo

Photo Credits: AP Images/Vincent Yu, 8; Shutterstock/Mikhail Nekrasov, 13

Design Elements: Shutterstock/Chen Ping Hung (framed edge design); mmmm (world map
design); Mushakesa (abstract lines design); Najin (old parchment design)

TABLE OF CONTENTS

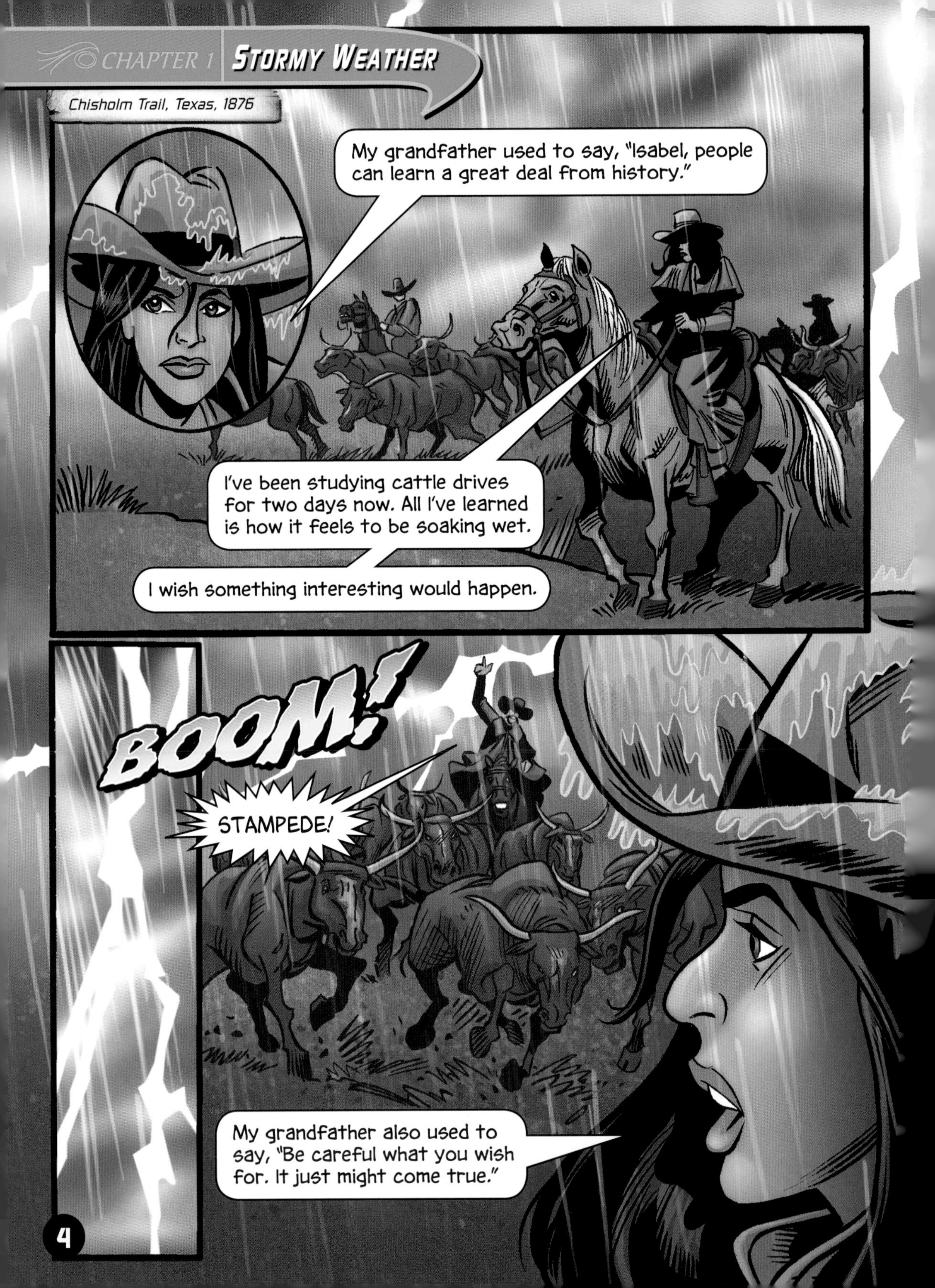
CHAPTER 1 STORMY WEATHER
Chisholm Trail, Texas, 1876
My grandfather used to say, "Isabel, people can learn a great deal from history."
I've been studying cattle drives for two days now. All I've learned is how it feels to be soaking wet.
I wish something interesting would happen.
BOOM!
STAMPEDE!
My grandfather also used to say, "Be careful what you wish for. It just might come true."

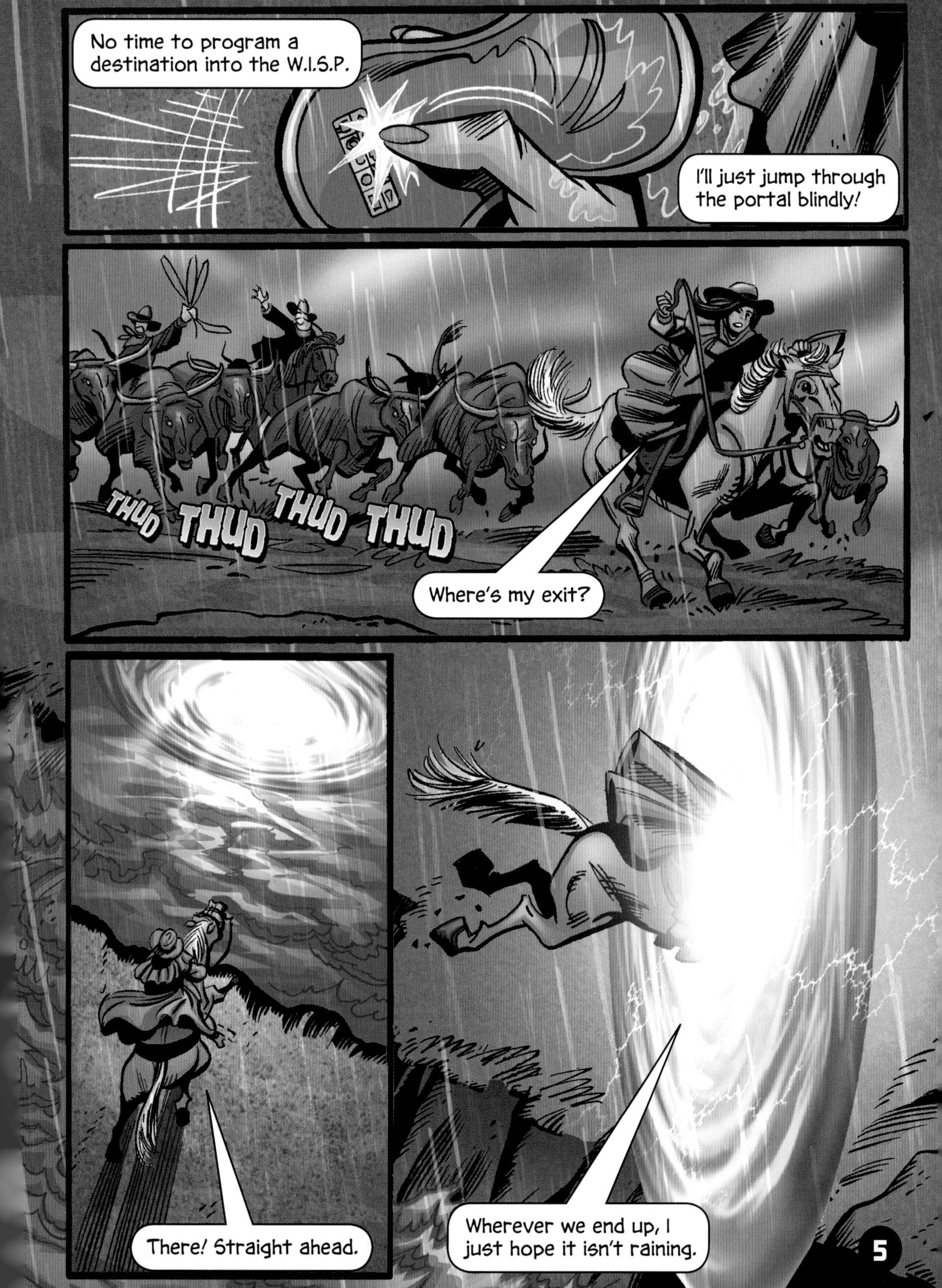
No time to program a destination into the W.I.S.P.
I'll just jump through the portal blindly!
THUD THUD THUD THUD
Where's my exit?
There! Straight ahead.
Wherever we end up, I just hope it isn't raining.

CHAPTER 2 **Out of the Frying Pan**

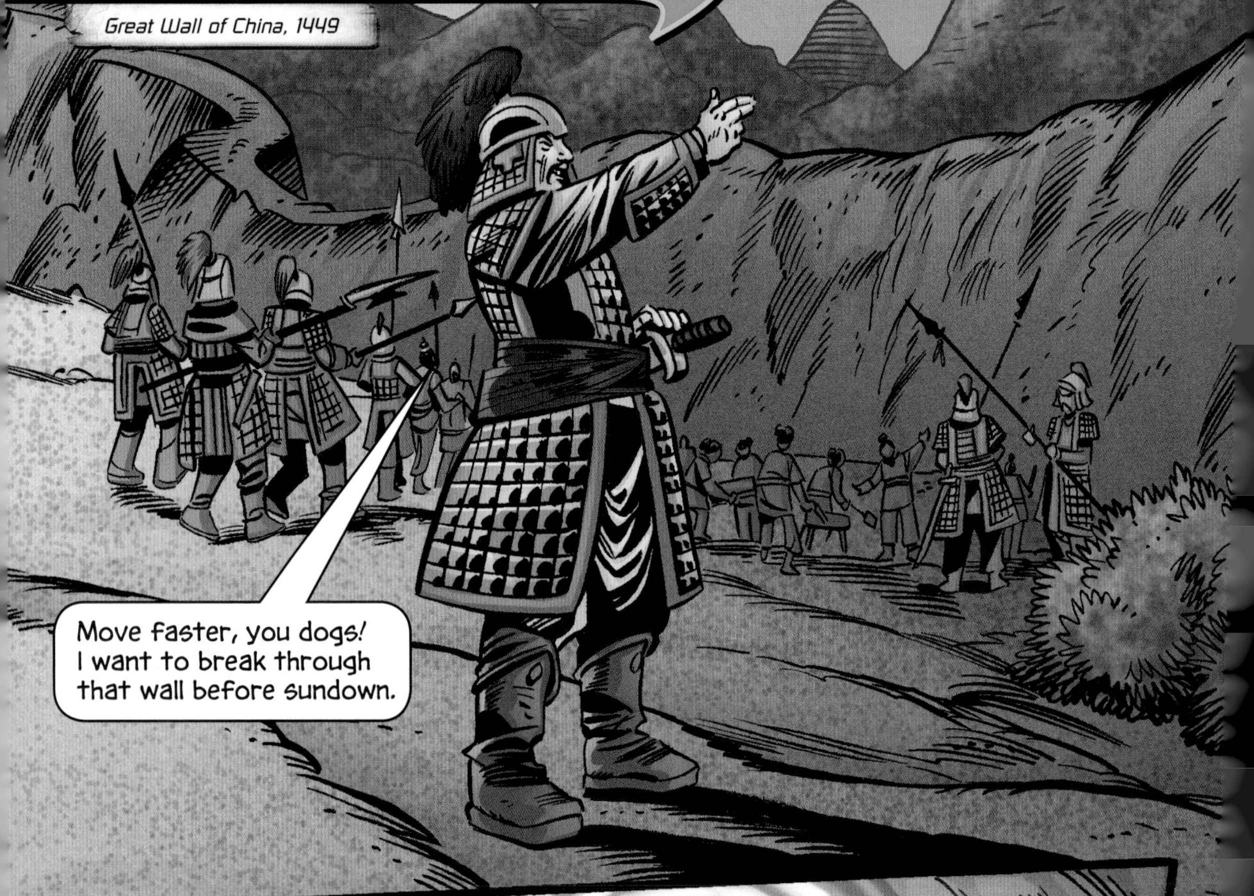
Great Wall of China, 1449
Move faster, you dogs! I want to break through that wall before sundown.

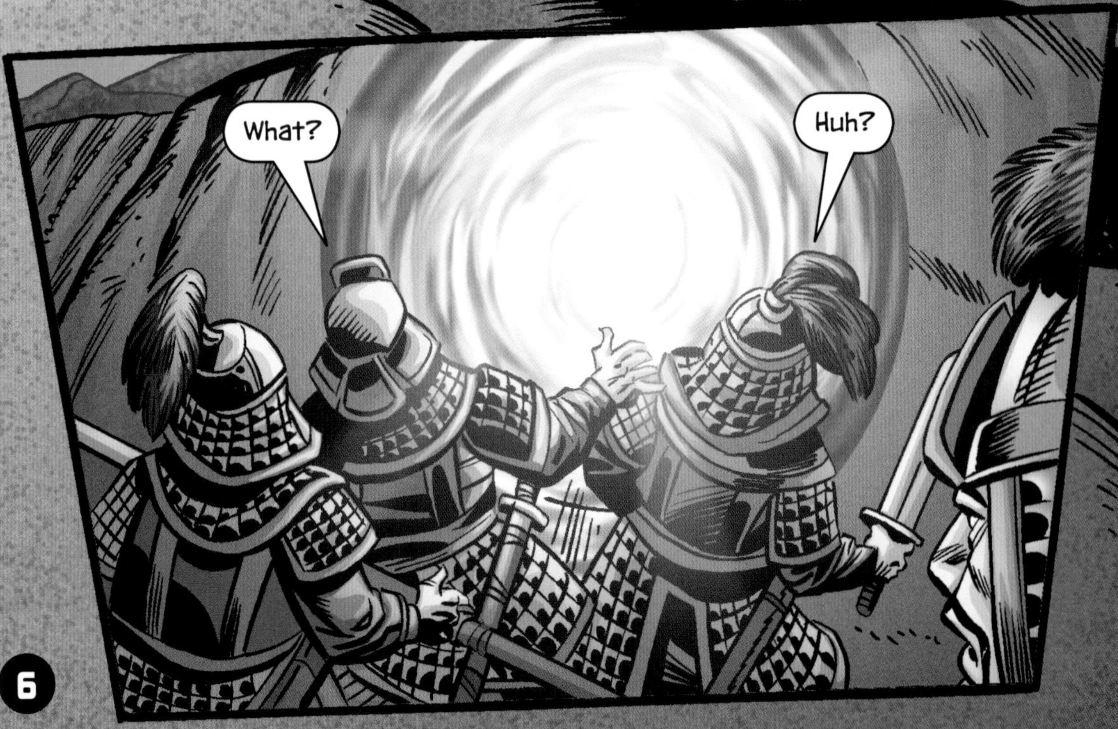
What?
Huh?

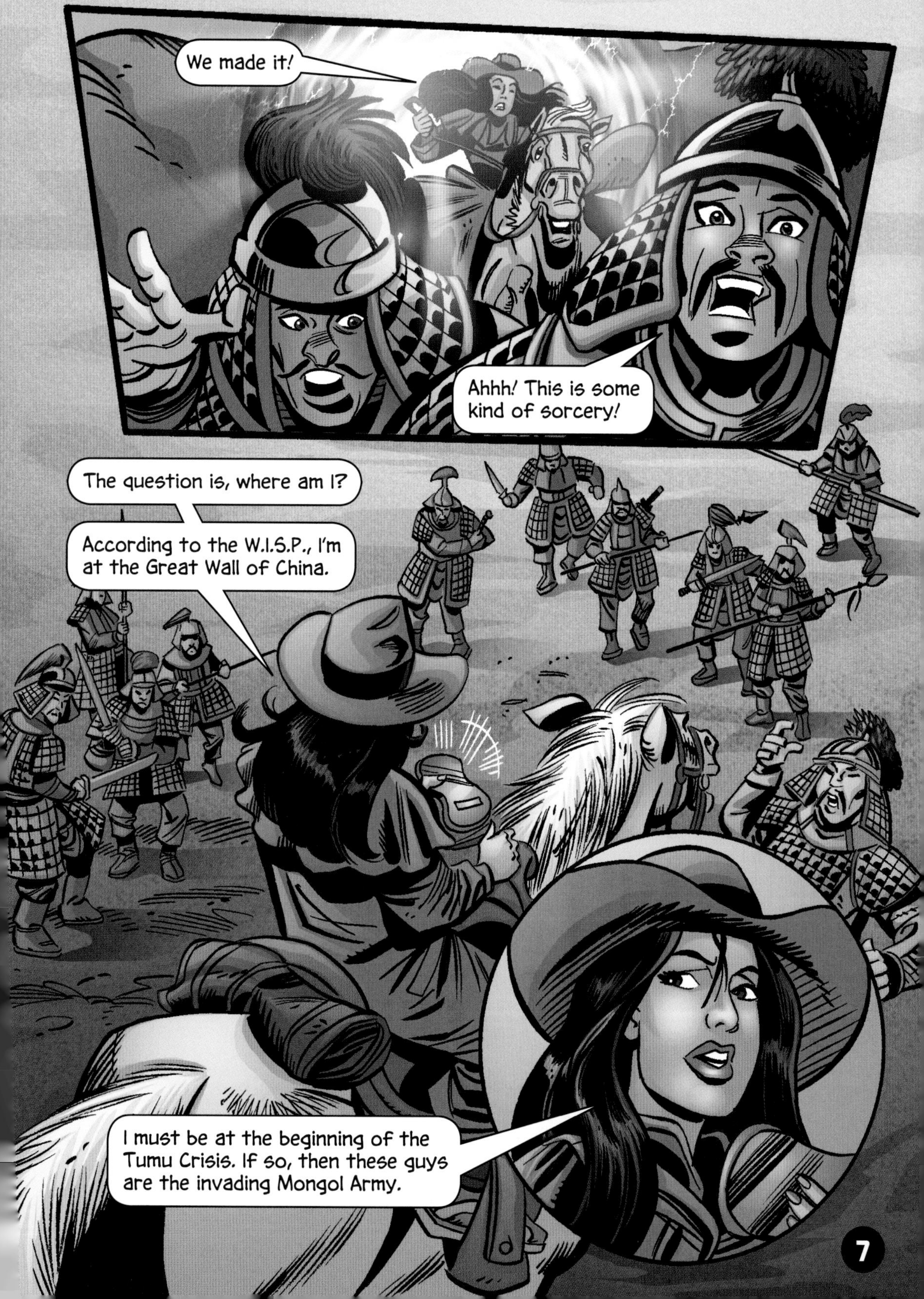
We made it!
Ahhh! This is some kind of sorcery!
The question is, where am I?
According to the W.I.S.P., I'm at the Great Wall of China.
I must be at the beginning of the Tumu Crisis. If so, then these guys are the invading Mongol Army.

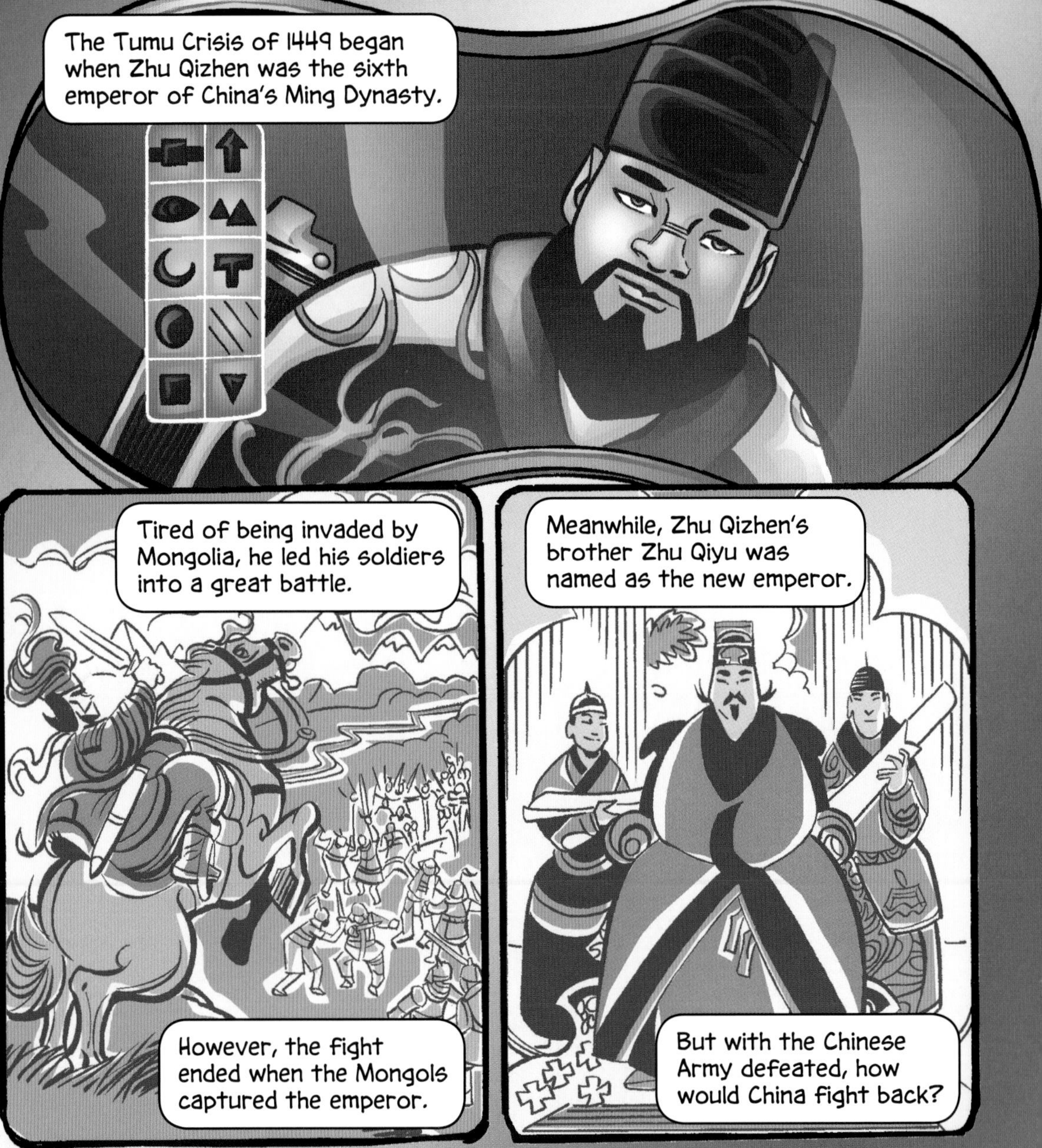
The Tumu Crisis of 1449 began when Zhu Qizhen was the sixth emperor of China's Ming Dynasty.
Tired of being invaded by Mongolia, he led his soldiers into a great battle.
However, the fight ended when the Mongols captured the emperor.
Meanwhile, Zhu Qizhen's brother Zhu Qiyu was named as the new emperor.
But with the Chinese Army defeated, how would China fight back?

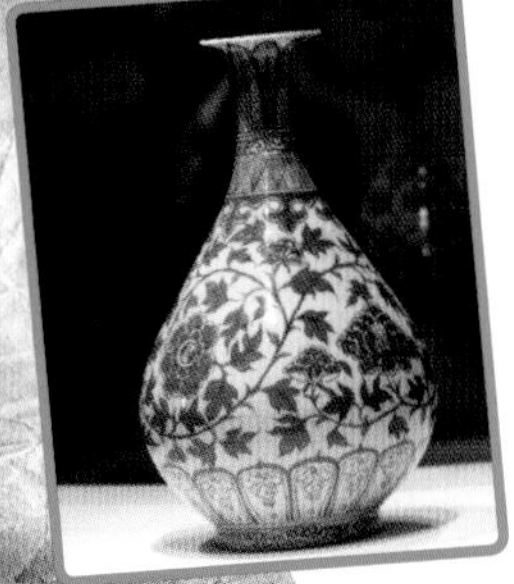

THE MING DYNASTY

The Ming Dynasty began ruling China in 1368. The dynasty was founded when the Han Chinese overthrew the Yuan Dynasty. The Ming Dynasty's government lasted 276 years. During that time, Chinese literature, art, and philosophy grew. The dynasty came to an end in 1644 when the Qing Dynasty rose to power.

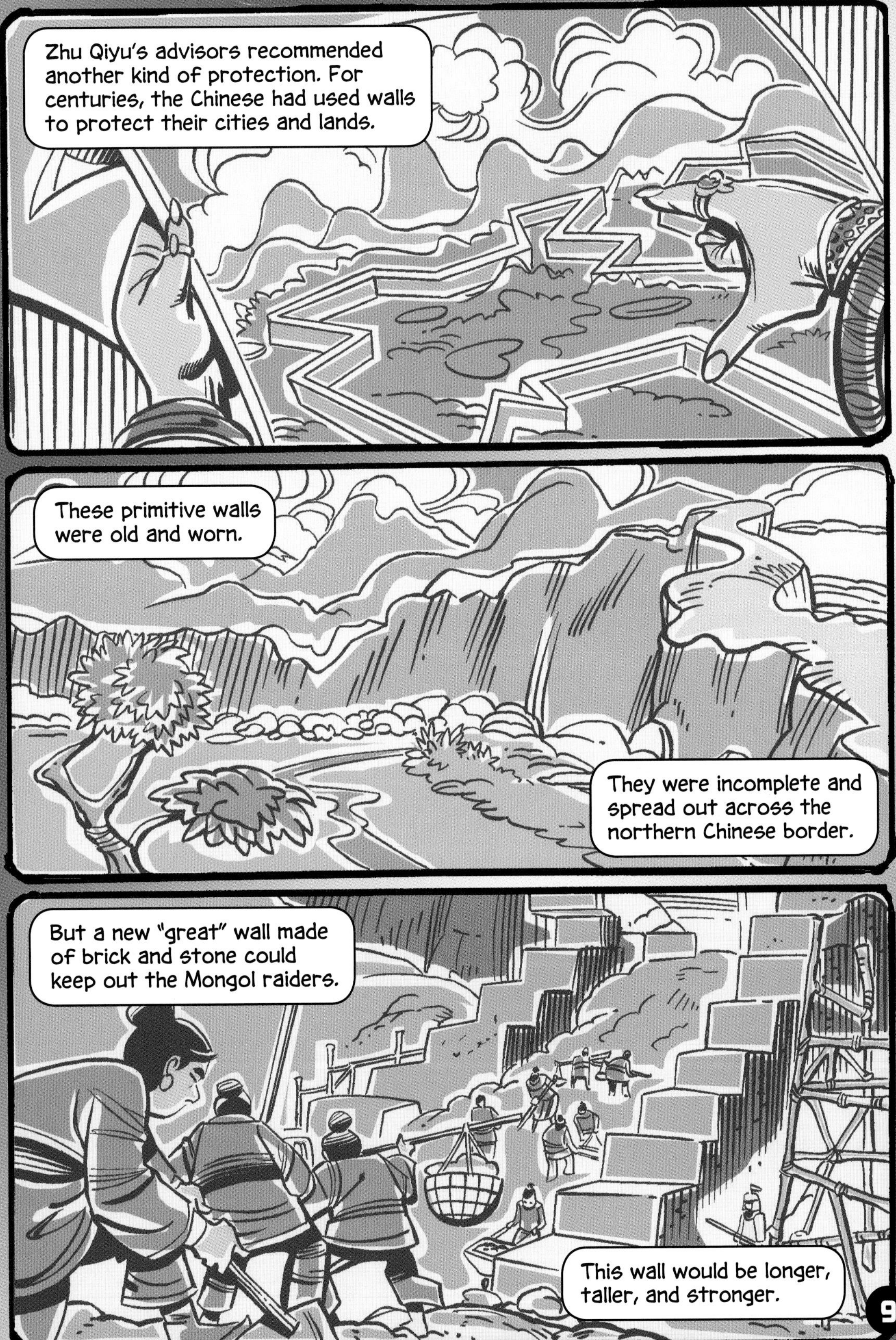
Zhu Qiyu's advisors recommended another kind of protection. For centuries, the Chinese had used walls to protect their cities and lands.
These primitive walls were old and worn.
They were incomplete and spread out across the northern Chinese border.
But a new "great" wall made of brick and stone could keep out the Mongol raiders.
This wall would be longer, taller, and stronger.

Now, what to do with my Mongol friends?
You jumped out of the wall itself! Are you woman or witch?
Either way, you cannot control us with your magic.
Control you with magic? We both know you are too powerful for such tricks.
I'm here to offer you a gift in return for my safety.
In my country, we have heard of the Mongols' horsemanship.

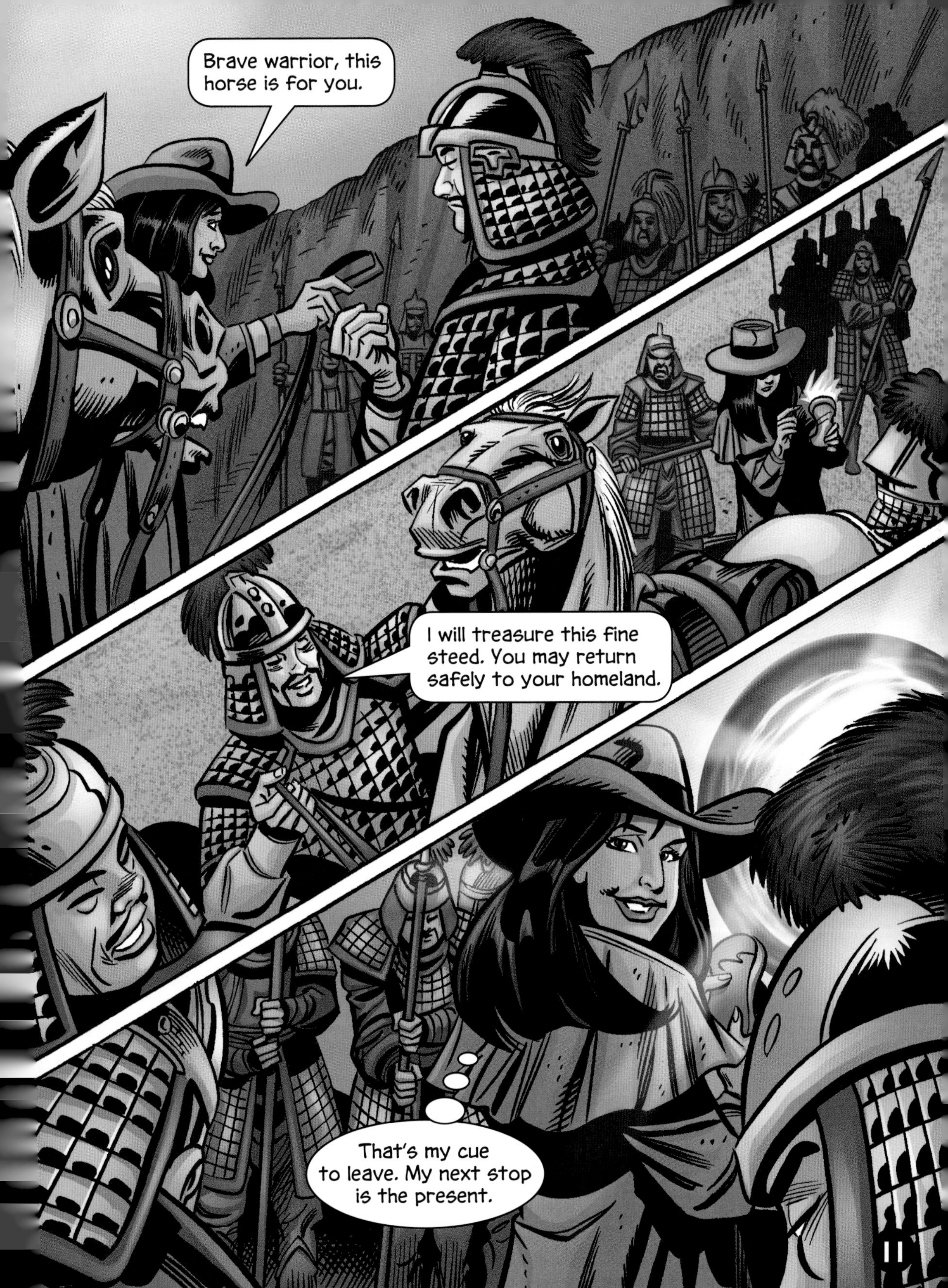
Brave warrior, this horse is for you.
I will treasure this fine steed. You may return safely to your homeland.
That's my cue to leave. My next stop is the present.

CHAPTER 3 Big Wall, Big Deal

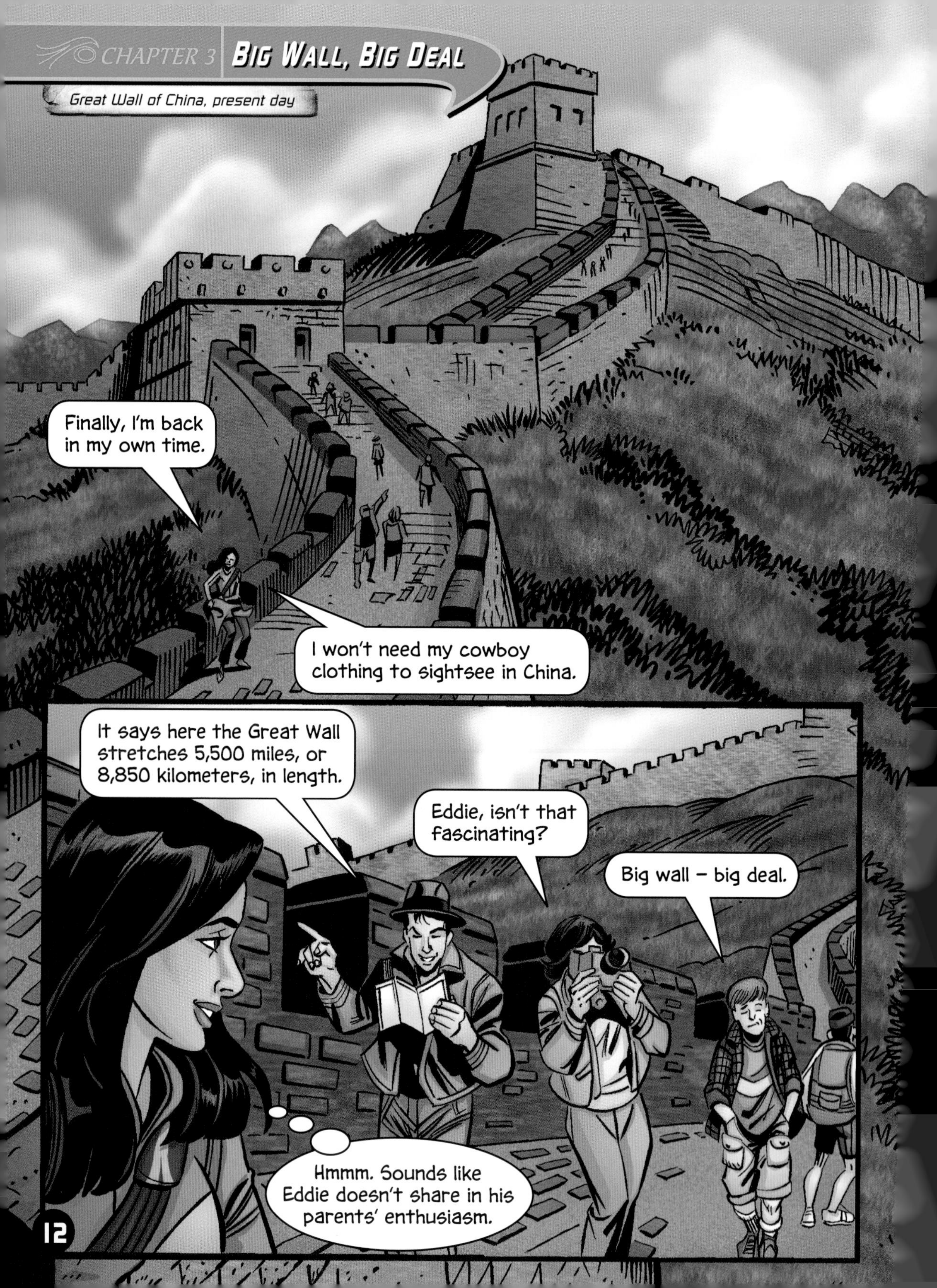
Great Wall of China, present day
Finally, I'm back in my own time.
I won't need my cowboy clothing to sightsee in China.
It says here the Great Wall stretches 5,500 miles, or 8,850 kilometers, in length.
Eddie, isn't that fascinating?
Big wall – big deal.
Hmmm. Sounds like Eddie doesn't share in his parents' enthusiasm.

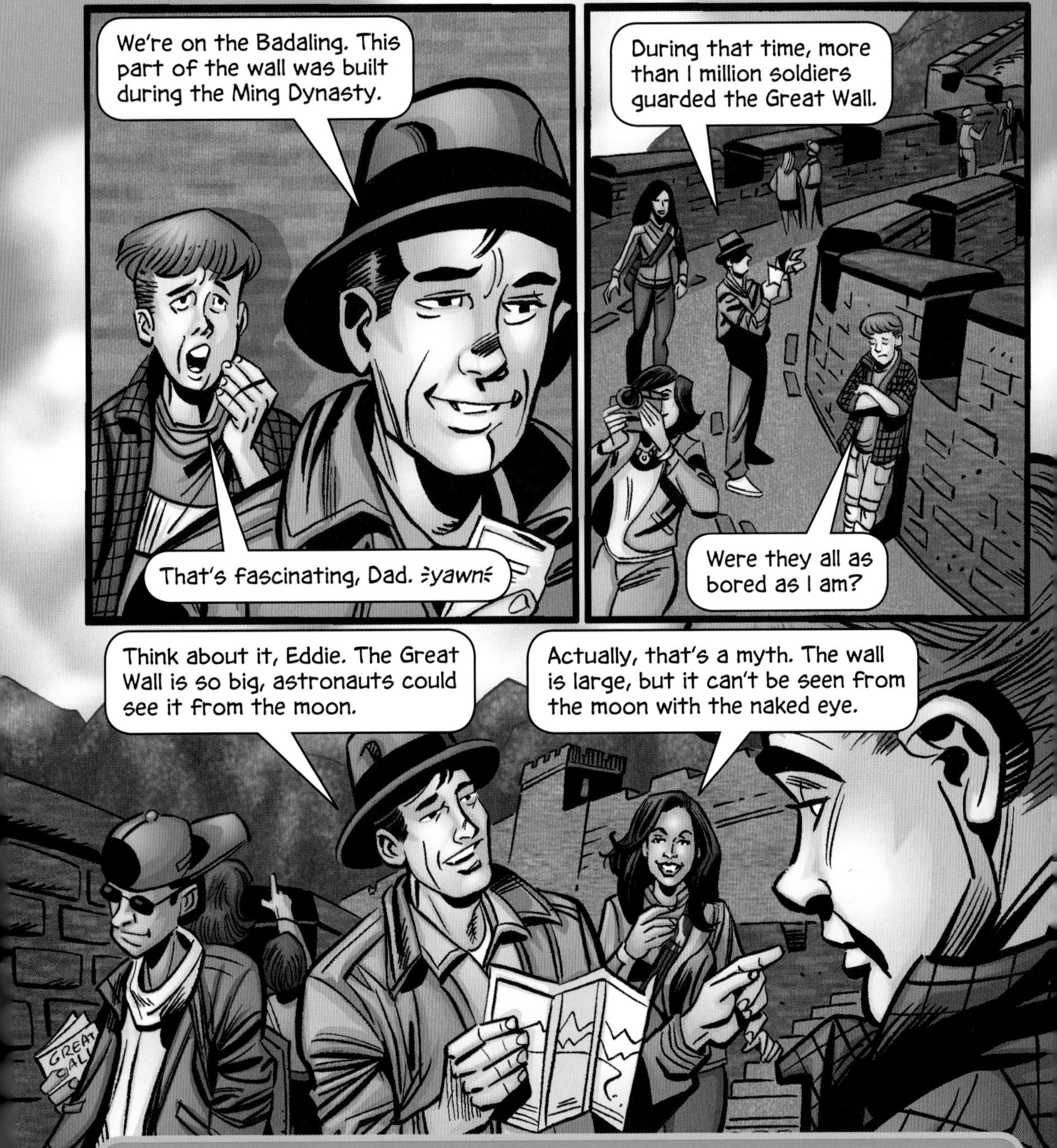
We're on the Badaling. This part of the wall was built during the Ming Dynasty.
That's fascinating, Dad. *yawn*
During that time, more than 1 million soldiers guarded the Great Wall.
Were they all as bored as I am?
Think about it, Eddie. The Great Wall is so big, astronauts could see it from the moon.
Actually, that's a myth. The wall is large, but it can't be seen from the moon with the naked eye.

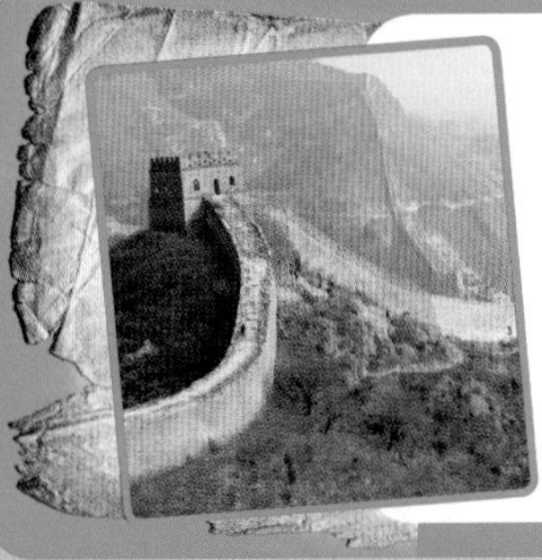

OTHER GREAT WALL MYTHS

Myth: The bodies of builders are buried inside the Great Wall.

Truth: Historians believe angry Chinese peasants started this myth because they were forced to work on the wall.

Myth: The Great Wall is one long wall with no breaks.

Truth: The wall stops and starts in several places.

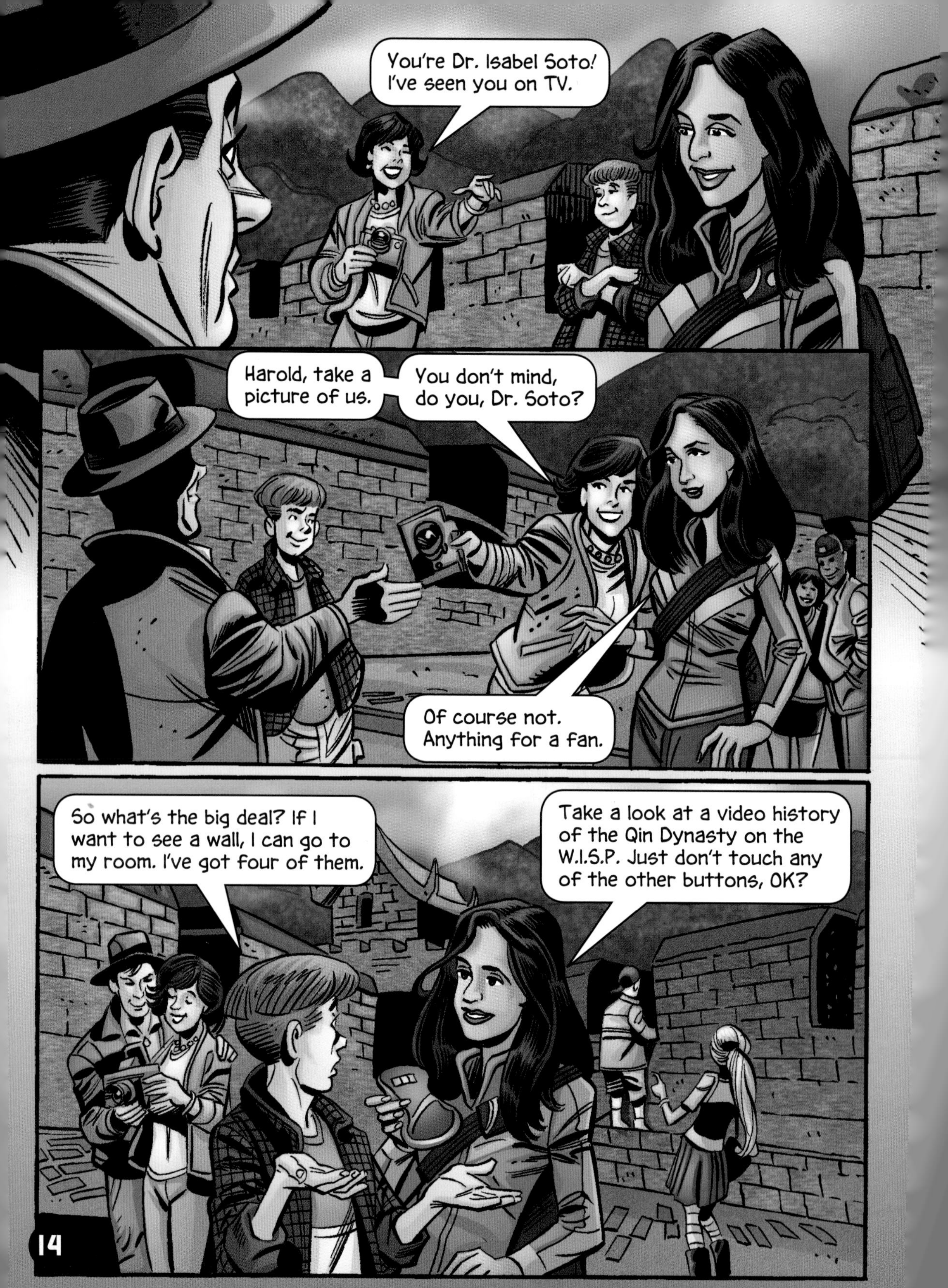
You're Dr. Isabel Soto! I've seen you on TV.
Harold, take a picture of us.
You don't mind, do you, Dr. Soto?
Of course not. Anything for a fan.
So what's the big deal? If I want to see a wall, I can go to my room. I've got four of them.
Take a look at a video history of the Qin Dynasty on the W.I.S.P. Just don't touch any of the other buttons, OK?

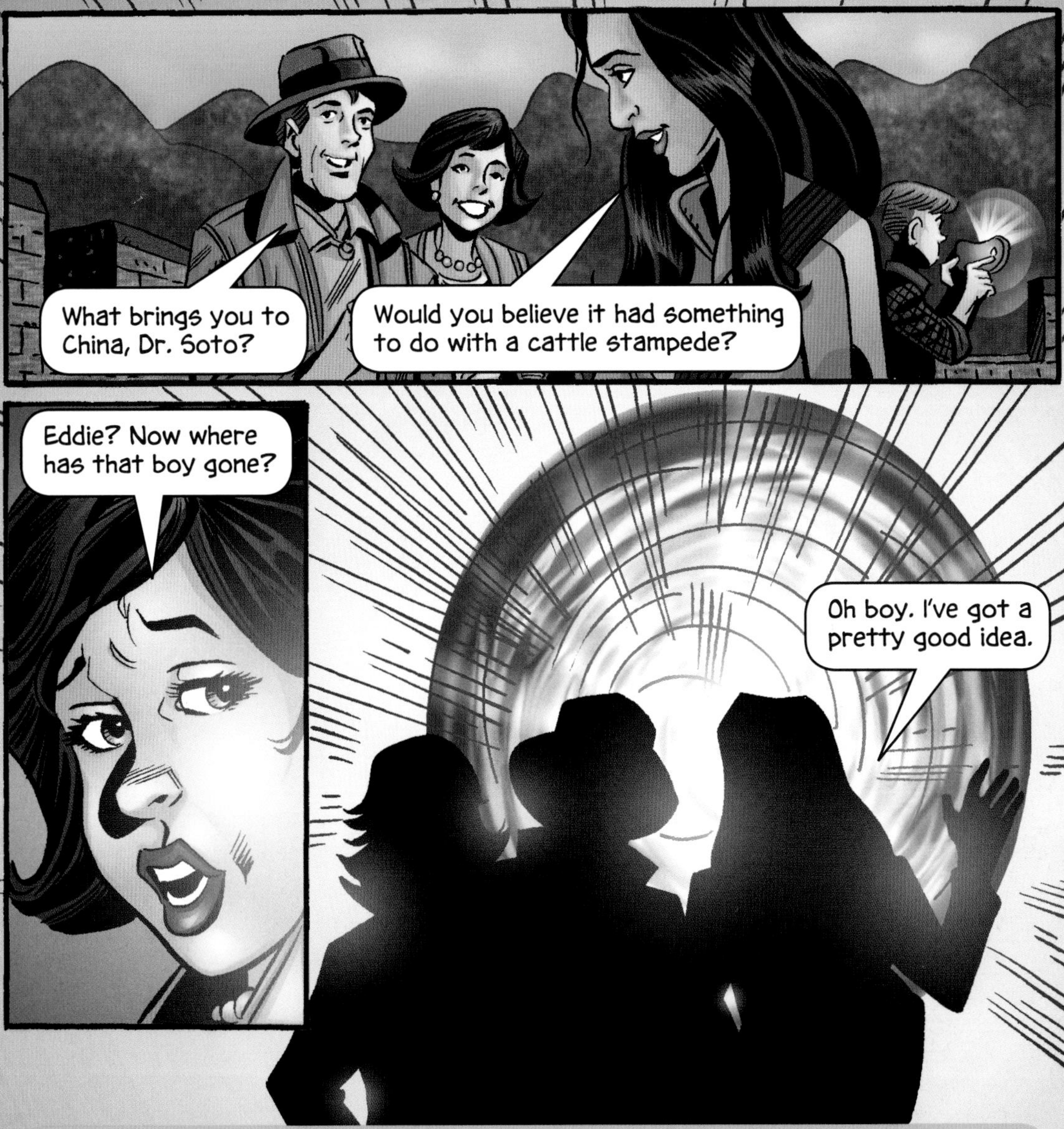
What brings you to China, Dr. Soto?
Would you believe it had something to do with a cattle stampede?
Eddie? Now where has that boy gone?
Oh boy. I've got a pretty good idea.

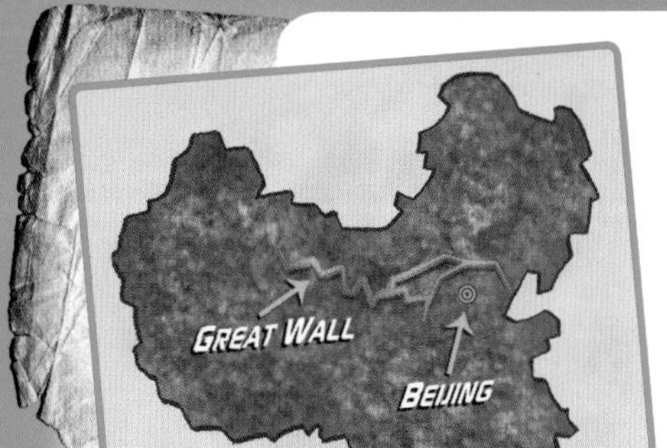
GREAT WALL
BEIJING

CHECK THE MAP

The Great Wall of China is the longest structure on earth made by humans. It has several different sections. Depending on what part of China is visited, the wall may be either unbroken or in ruins. Vandals have damaged many parts of the wall. Other parts of the wall have been knocked down for new construction projects. People have even stolen bricks to build their own homes.

CHAPTER 4 WALL-TO-WALL

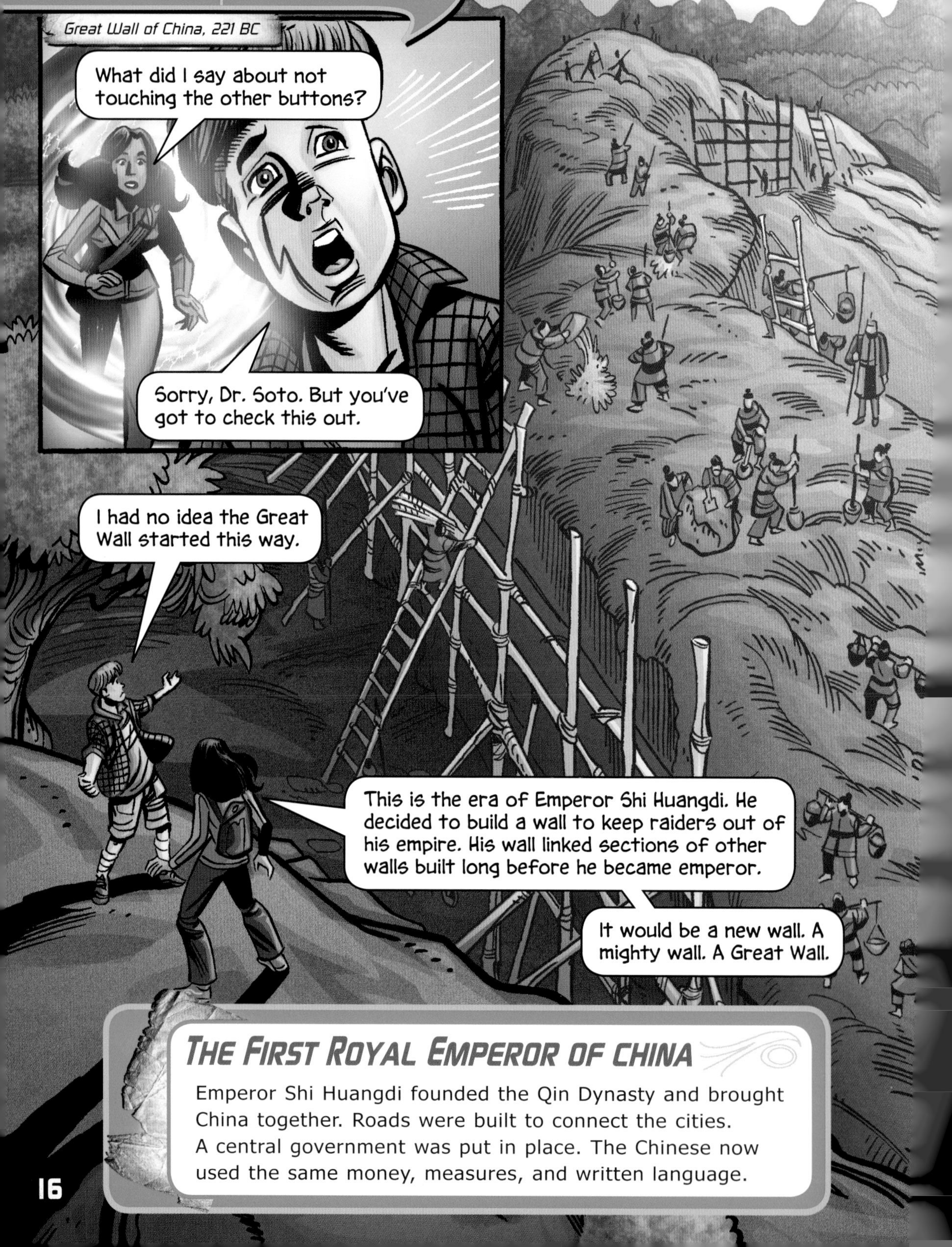
Great Wall of China, 221 BC
What did I say about not touching the other buttons?
Sorry, Dr. Soto. But you've got to check this out.
I had no idea the Great Wall started this way.
This is the era of Emperor Shi Huangdi. He decided to build a wall to keep raiders out of his empire. His wall linked sections of other walls built long before he became emperor.
It would be a new wall. A mighty wall. A Great Wall.

THE FIRST ROYAL EMPEROR OF CHINA

Emperor Shi Huangdi founded the Qin Dynasty and brought China together. Roads were built to connect the cities. A central government was put in place. The Chinese now used the same money, measures, and written language.

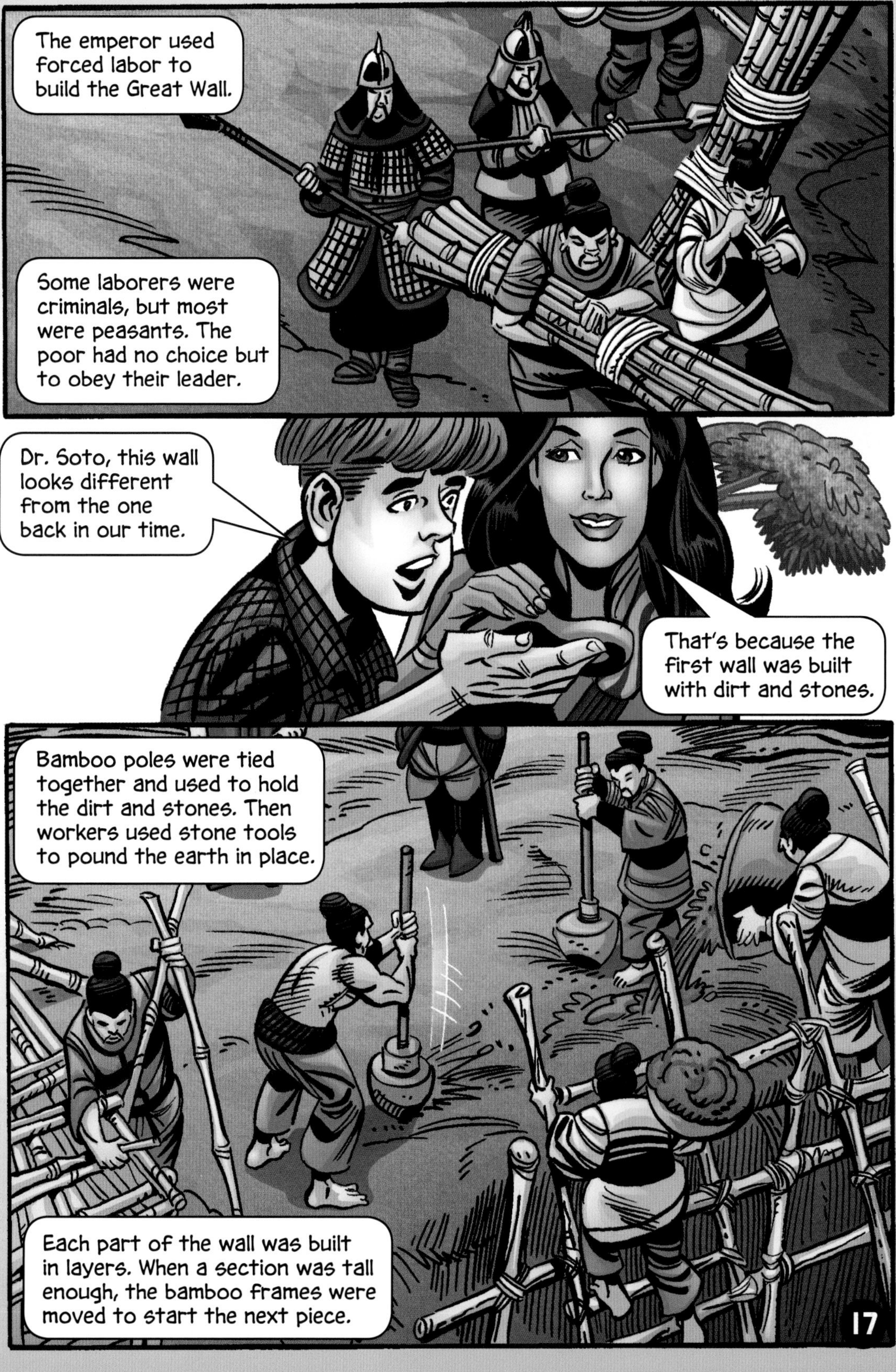
The emperor used forced labor to build the Great Wall.
Some laborers were criminals, but most were peasants. The poor had no choice but to obey their leader.
Dr. Soto, this wall looks different from the one back in our time.
That's because the first wall was built with dirt and stones.
Bamboo poles were tied together and used to hold the dirt and stones. Then workers used stone tools to pound the earth in place.
Each part of the wall was built in layers. When a section was tall enough, the bamboo frames were moved to start the next piece.

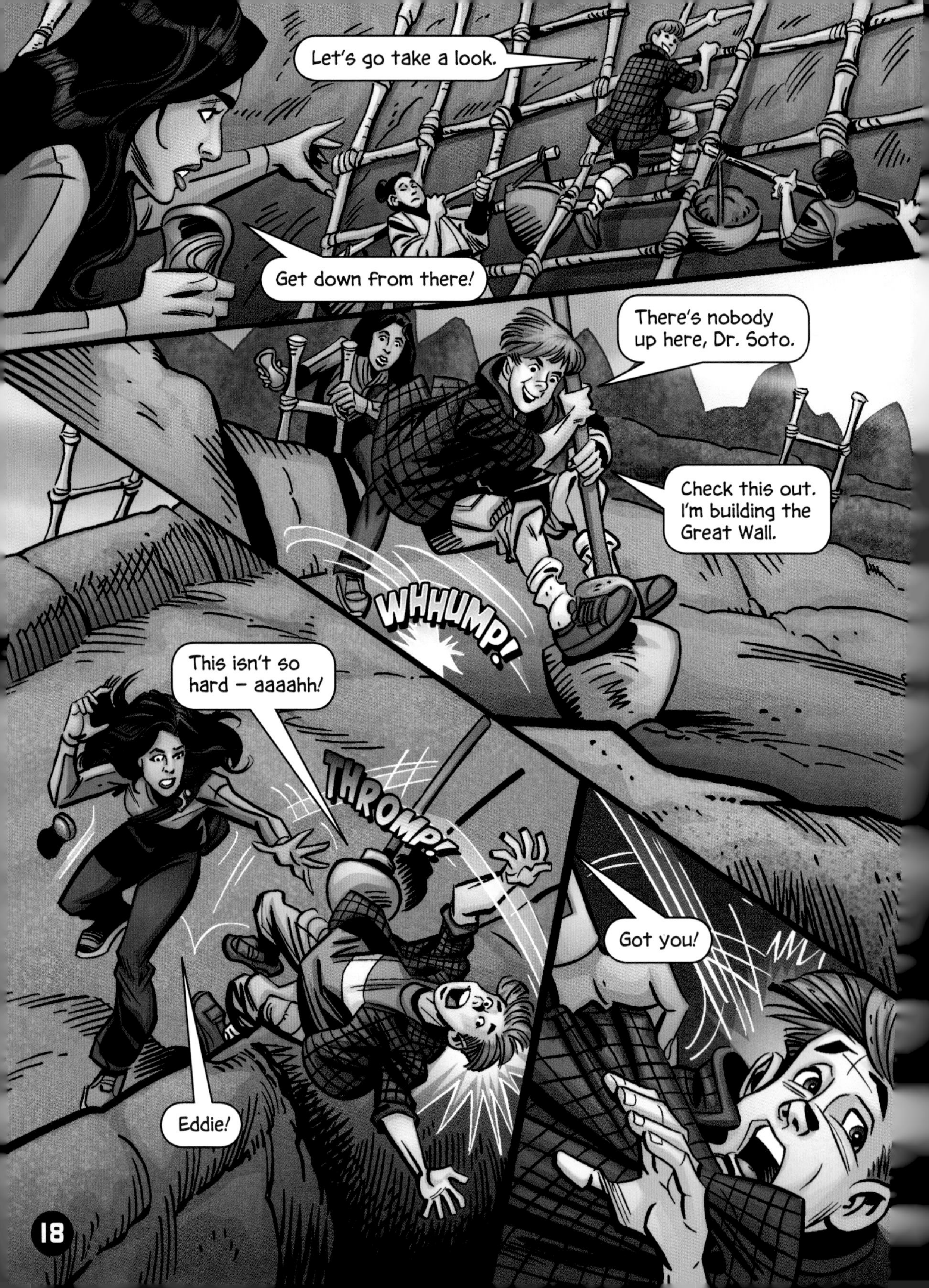
Let's go take a look.
Get down from there!
There's nobody up here, Dr. Soto.
Check this out. I'm building the Great Wall.
WHHUMP!
This isn't so hard – aaaahh!
THROMP!
Eddie!
Got you!

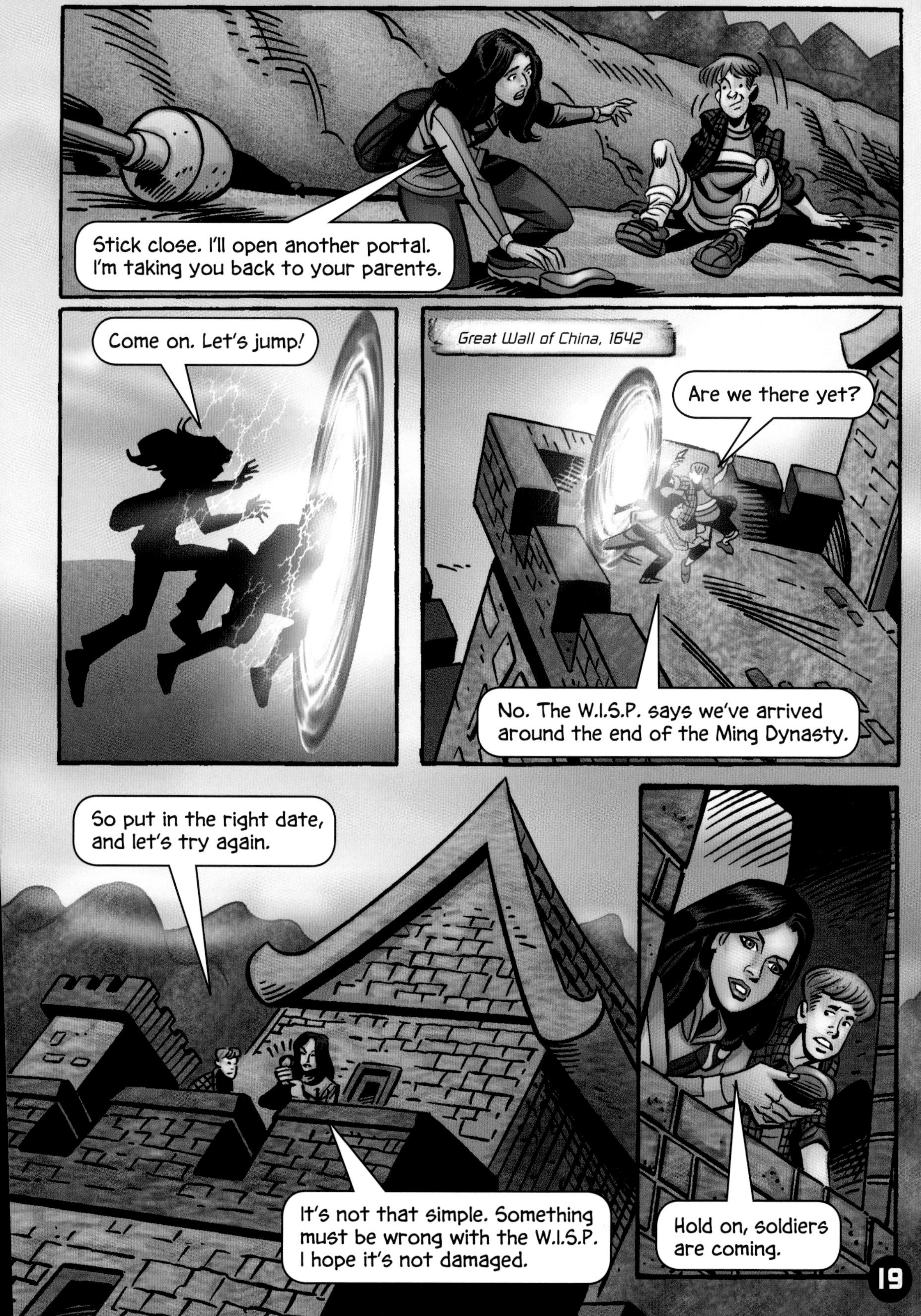
Stick close. I'll open another portal.
I'm taking you back to your parents.
Come on. Let's jump!
Great Wall of China, 1642
Are we there yet?
No. The W.I.S.P. says we've arrived around the end of the Ming Dynasty.
So put in the right date, and let's try again.
It's not that simple. Something must be wrong with the W.I.S.P. I hope it's not damaged.
Hold on, soldiers are coming.

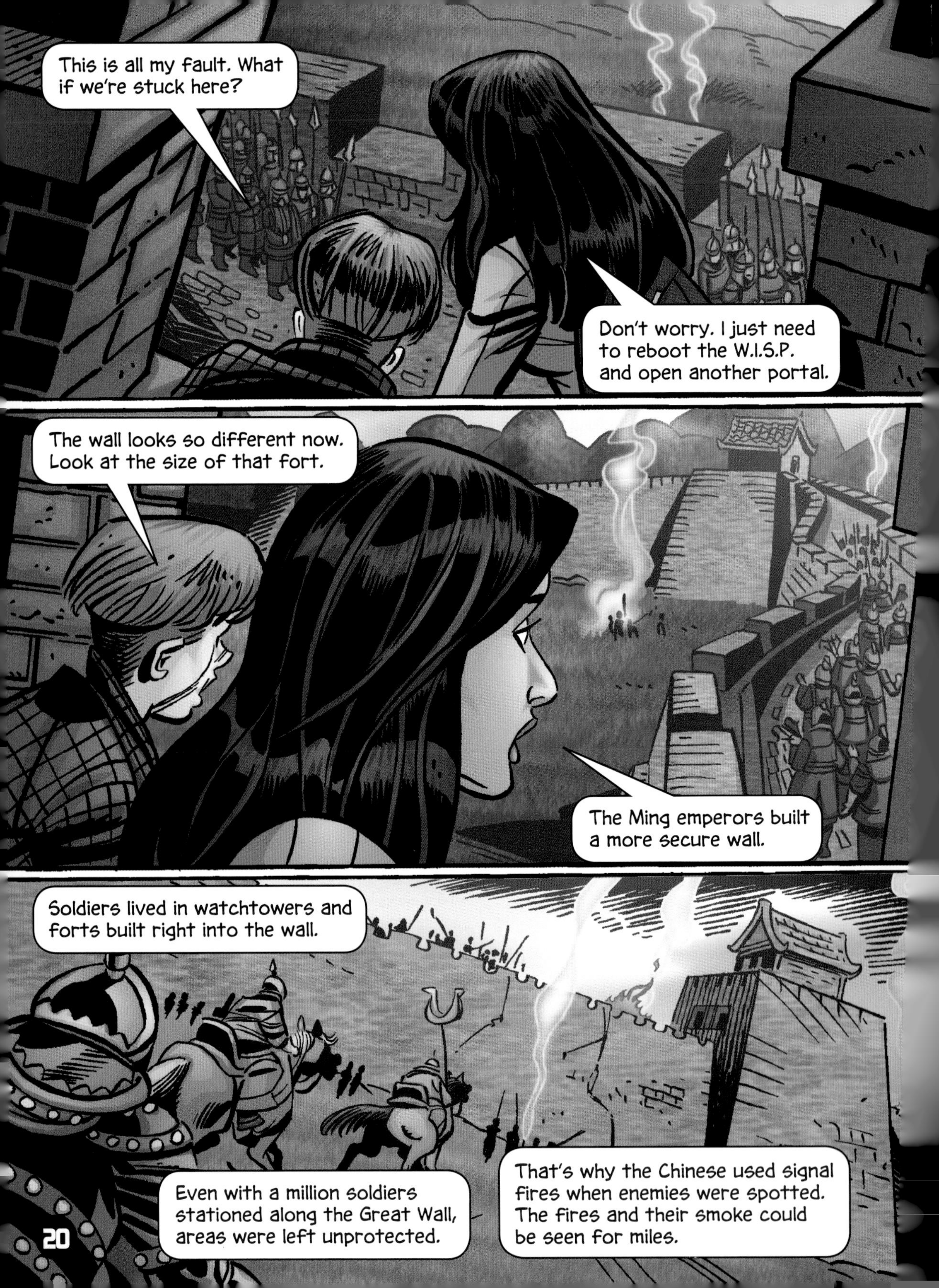
This is all my fault. What if we're stuck here?
Don't worry. I just need to reboot the W.I.S.P. and open another portal.
The wall looks so different now. Look at the size of that fort.
The Ming emperors built a more secure wall.
Soldiers lived in watchtowers and forts built right into the wall.
Even with a million soldiers stationed along the Great Wall, areas were left unprotected.
That's why the Chinese used signal fires when enemies were spotted. The fires and their smoke could be seen for miles.

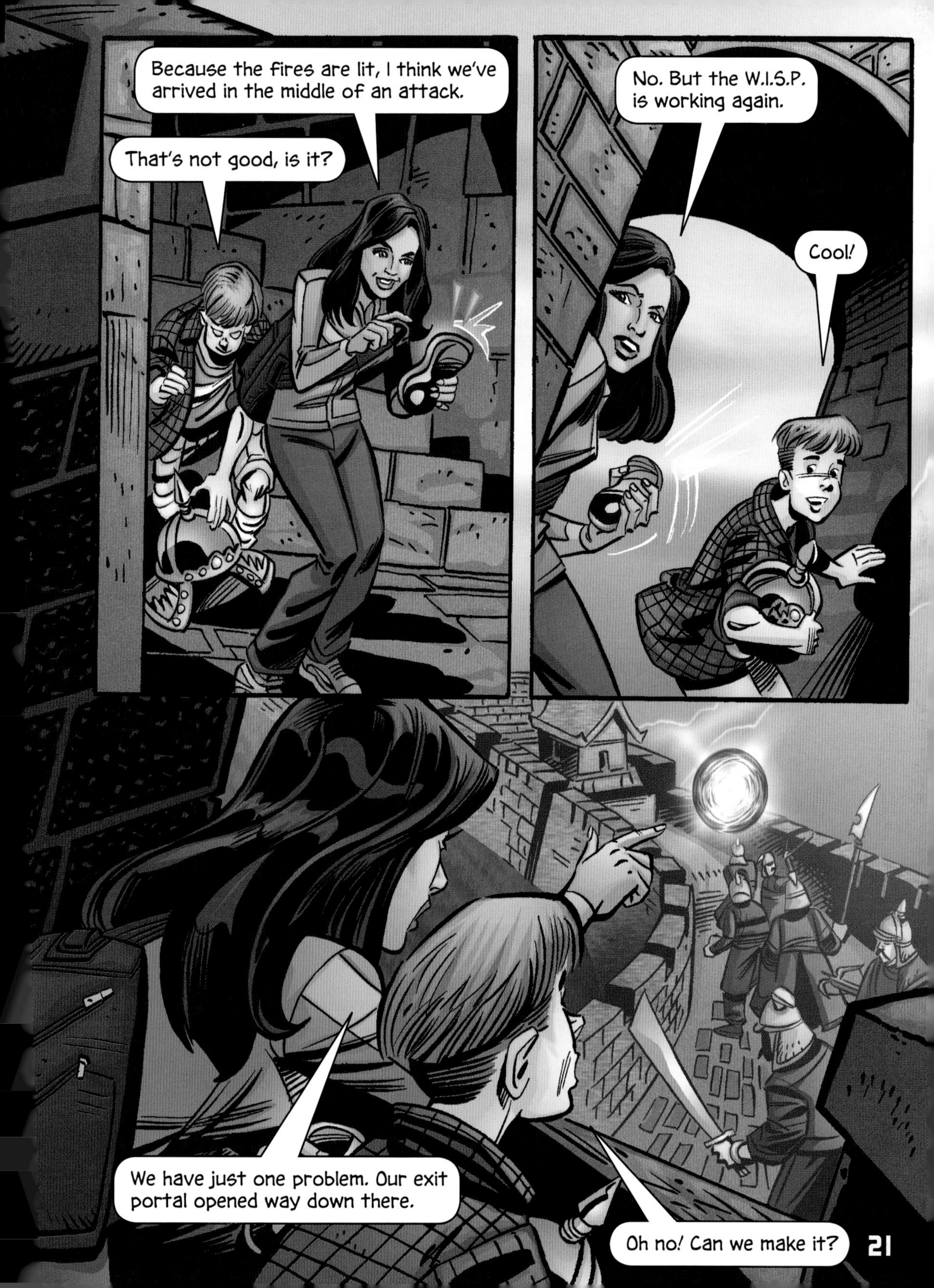
Because the fires are lit, I think we've arrived in the middle of an attack.
That's not good, is it?
No. But the W.I.S.P. is working again.
Cool!
We have just one problem. Our exit portal opened way down there.
Oh no! Can we make it?

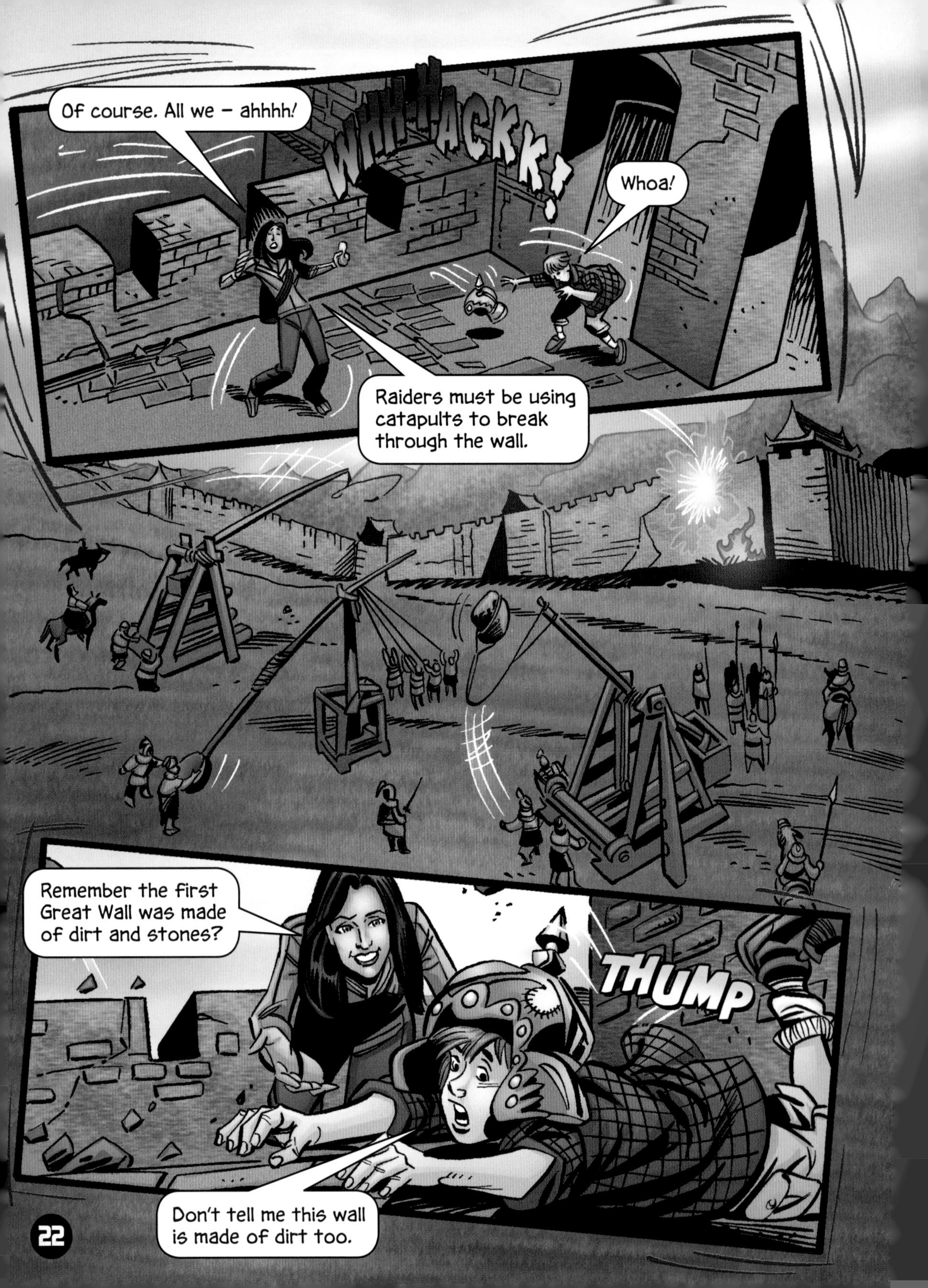
Of course. All we – ahhhh!
WHH-HACKK!
Whoa!
Raiders must be using catapults to break through the wall.
Remember the first Great Wall was made of dirt and stones?
THUMP
Don't tell me this wall is made of dirt too.

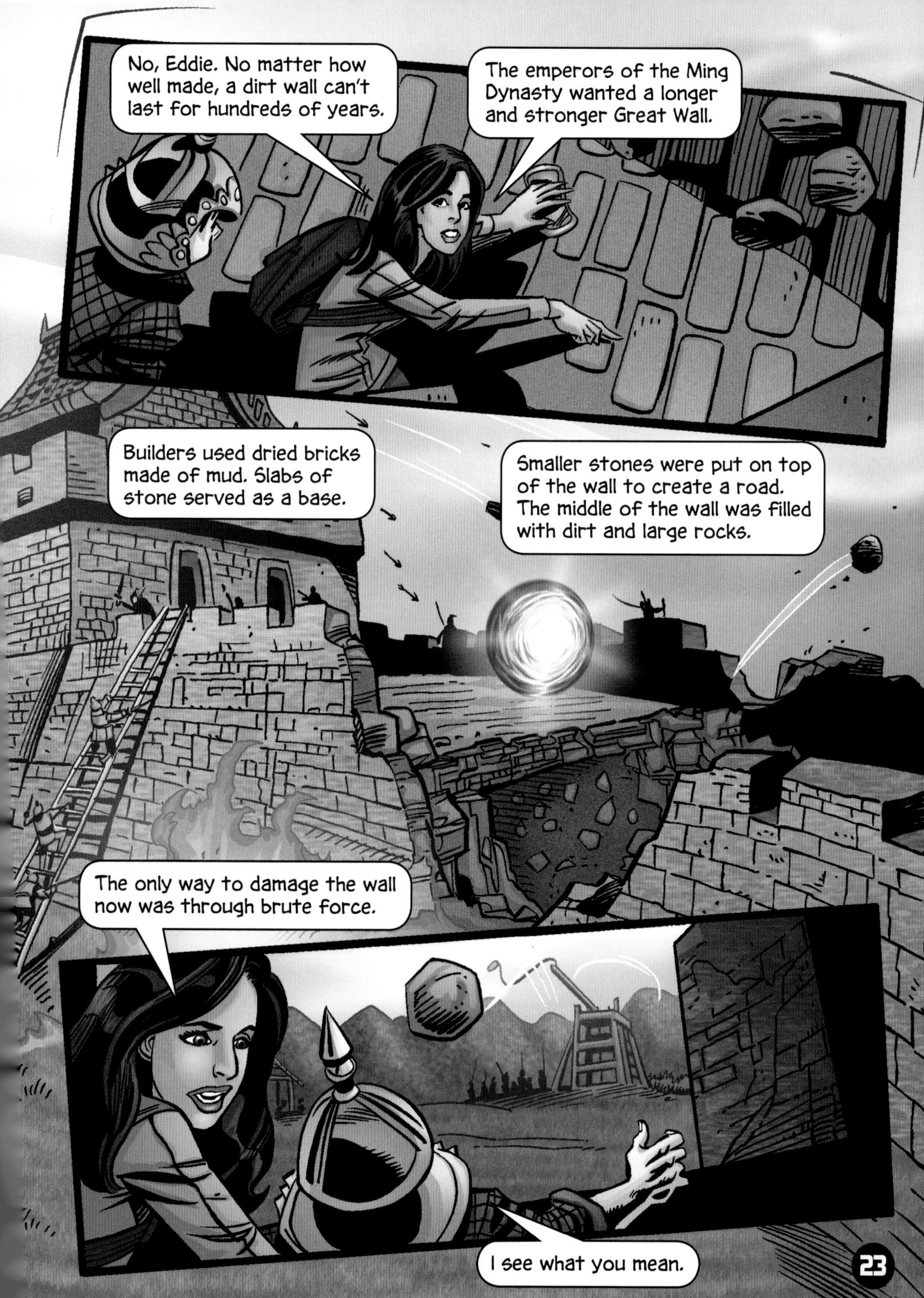
No, Eddie. No matter how well made, a dirt wall can't last for hundreds of years.
The emperors of the Ming Dynasty wanted a longer and stronger Great Wall.
Builders used dried bricks made of mud. Slabs of stone served as a base.
Smaller stones were put on top of the wall to create a road. The middle of the wall was filled with dirt and large rocks.
The only way to damage the wall now was through brute force.
I see what you mean.

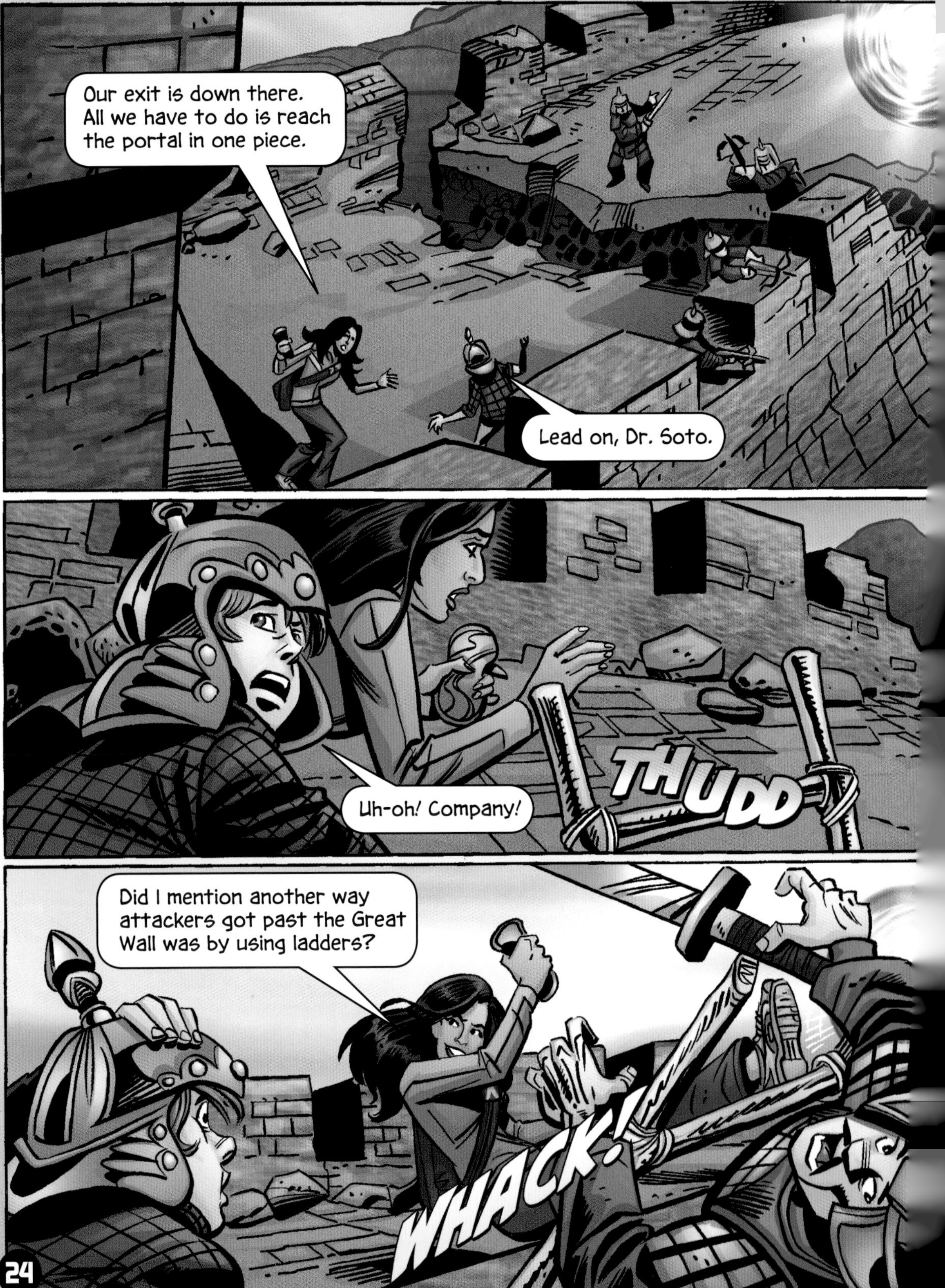
Our exit is down there. All we have to do is reach the portal in one piece.
Lead on, Dr. Soto.
Uh-oh! Company!
THUDD
Did I mention another way attackers got past the Great Wall was by using ladders?
WHACK!

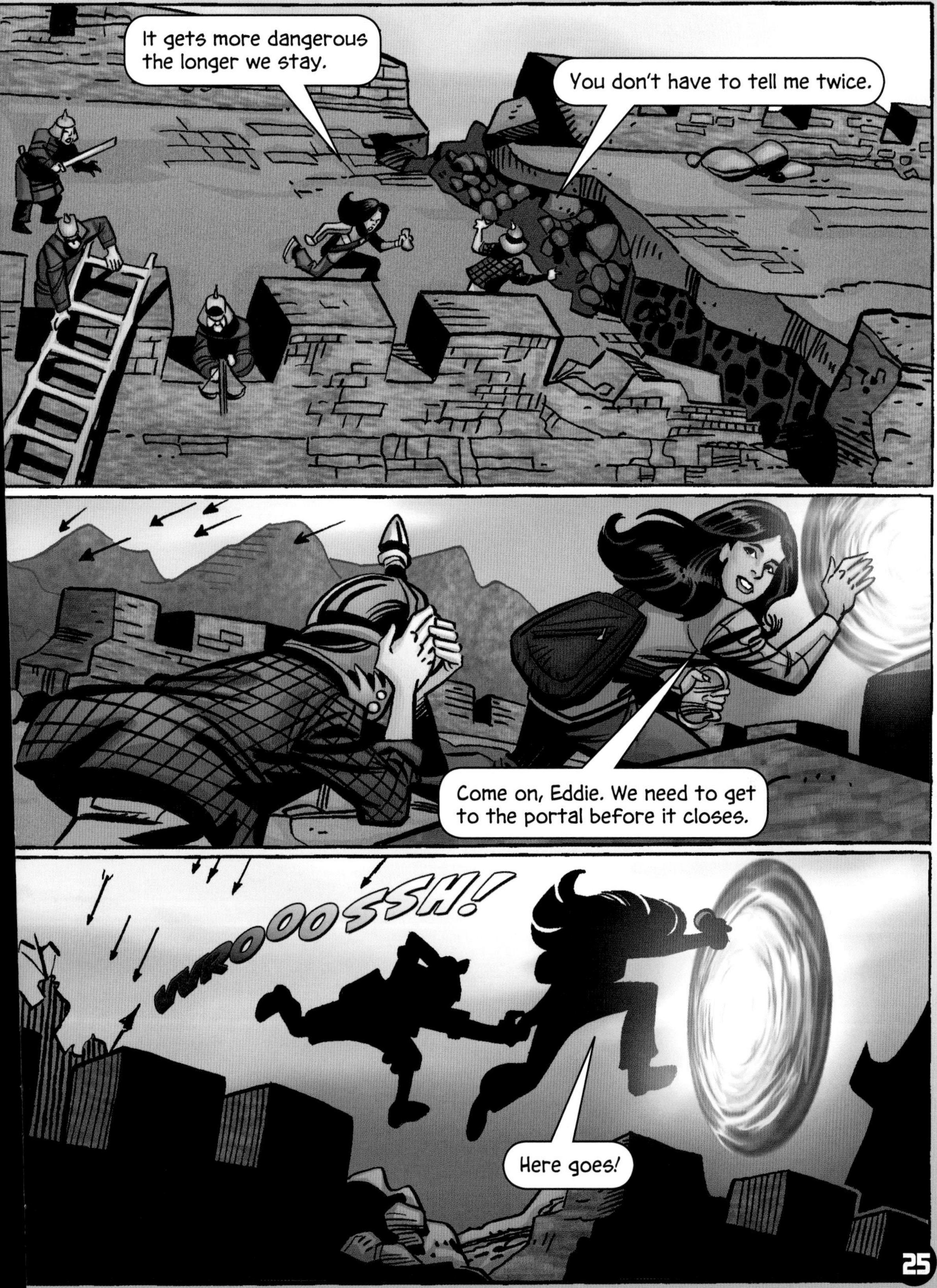
It gets more dangerous the longer we stay.
You don't have to tell me twice.
Come on, Eddie. We need to get to the portal before it closes.
WROOOSSH!
Here goes!

CHAPTER 5 An Amazing Achievement

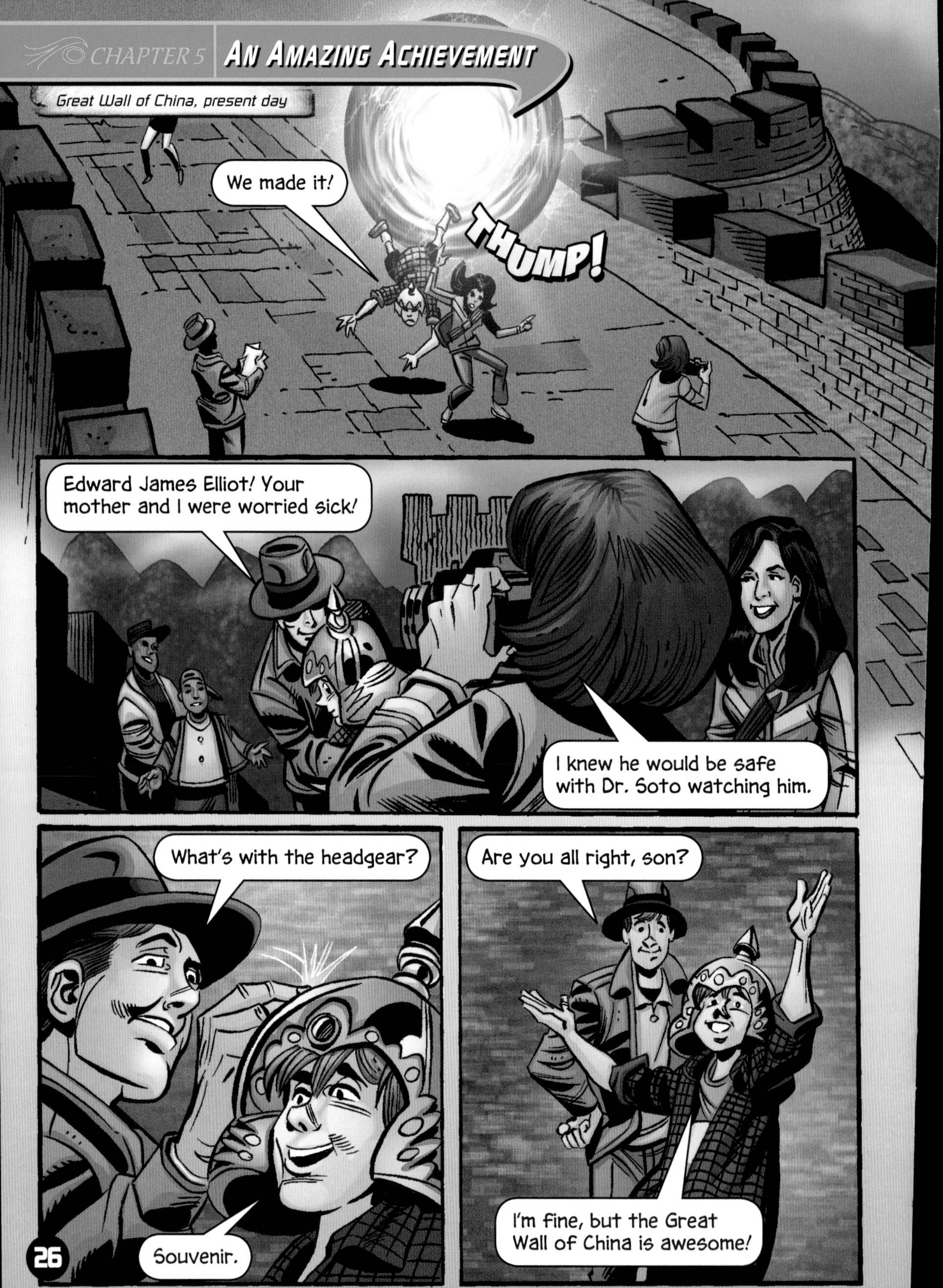

Great Wall of China, present day
We made it!
THUMP!
Edward James Elliot! Your mother and I were worried sick!
I knew he would be safe with Dr. Soto watching him.
What's with the headgear?
Souvenir.
Are you all right, son?
I'm fine, but the Great Wall of China is awesome!

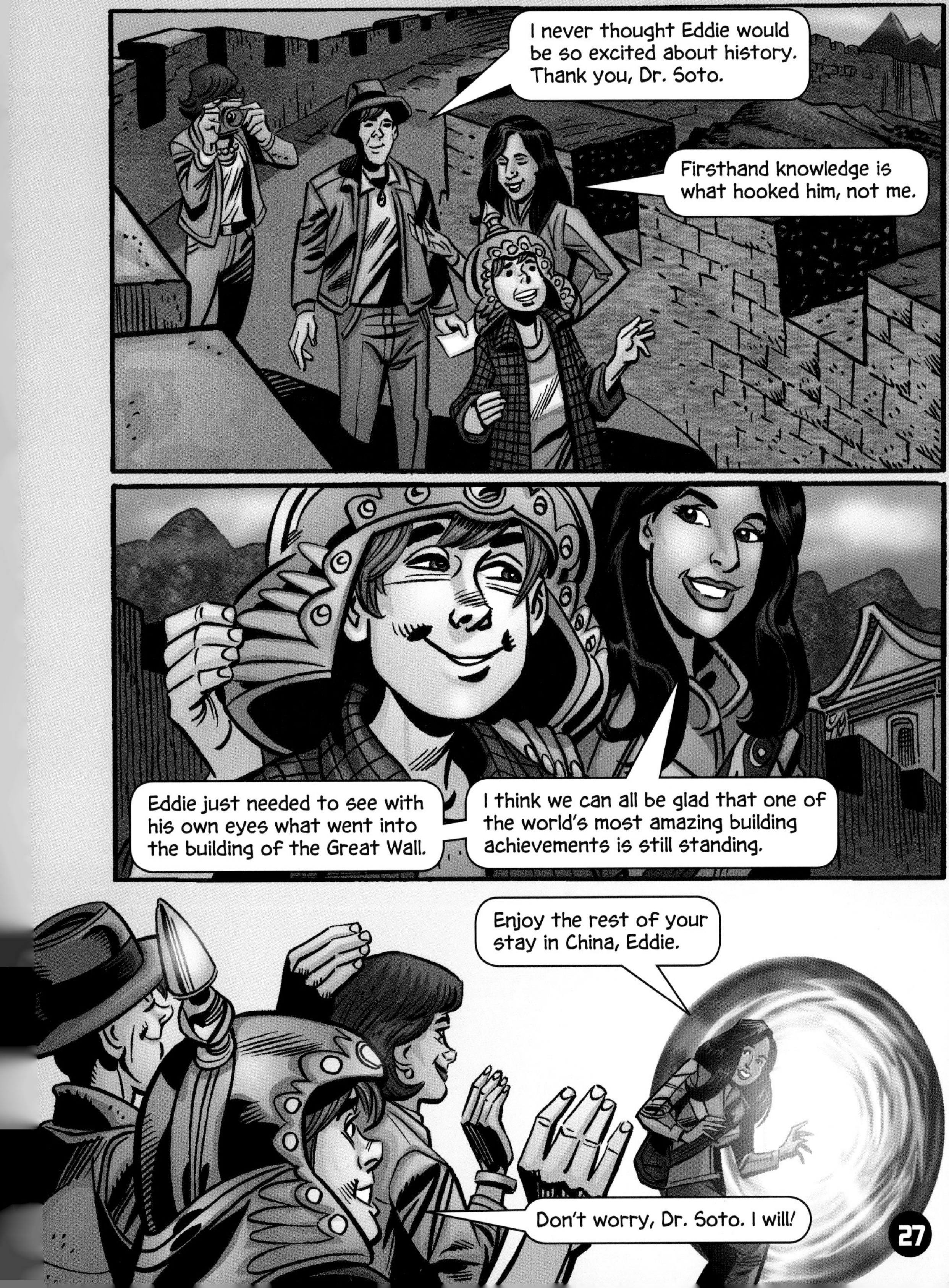
I never thought Eddie would be so excited about history. Thank you, Dr. Soto.
Firsthand knowledge is what hooked him, not me.
Eddie just needed to see with his own eyes what went into the building of the Great Wall.
I think we can all be glad that one of the world's most amazing building achievements is still standing.
Enjoy the rest of your stay in China, Eddie.
Don't worry, Dr. Soto. I will!

MORE ABOUT THE GREAT WALL

- During the Qin Dynasty, about one out of every 20 people in China worked on the Great Wall. It was during this same dynasty that the word "China" was created.

- Building the Great Wall was very expensive. To pay for the materials, the Chinese government raised taxes on the poor. This tax caused many citizens to dislike the wall.

- The average height of the Great Wall is 25 feet (8 meters). The width of the wall ranges from 15 to 25 feet (5 to 8 meters). Along most sections, a 13-foot- (4-meter-) wide roadway runs along the top of the wall.

- The Great Wall was built to defend China from raiders and other invaders. Today the wall serves as a popular tourist destination. Each year, more than 10 million tourists visit the Great Wall.

- The Badaling is one of the most visited sections of the Great Wall. This section was built during the Ming Dynasty. It is located about 43 miles (69 kilometers) north of China's capital of Beijing. The Badaling section is famous for the way the Great Wall snakes up and down mountain slopes.

- On June 25, 1899, a hoax appeared in newspapers across the United States. In this fake story, rumors flew about American businessmen planning to tear down the Great Wall. They would then build a road in its place to help the Chinese economy.

On February 24, 1972, Richard Nixon made history as the first U.S. president to visit the Great Wall. During his visit, President Nixon said, "Only a great nation can build such a magnificent Great Wall."

The Great Wall Marathon is a race held in Tianjin, China. The challenging race requires runners to run alongside and on top of the Great Wall. Runners must climb 5,164 steps going both up and down the wall.

MORE ABOUT

Isabel Soto

NAME: Dr. Isabel "Izzy" Soto
DEGREES: History and Anthropology
BUILD: Athletic HAIR: Dark Brown
EYES: Brown HEIGHT: 5′7″

W.I.S.P.: The Worldwide Inter-dimensional Space/Time Portal developed by Max Axiom at Axiom Laboratory.

BACKSTORY: Dr. Isabel "Izzy" Soto caught the history bug as a little girl. Every night, her grandfather told her about his adventures exploring ancient ruins in South America. He believed lost cultures teach people a great deal about history.

Izzy's love of cultures followed her to college. She studied history and anthropology. On a research trip to Thailand, she discovered an ancient stone with mysterious energy. Izzy took the stone to Super Scientist Max Axiom, who determined that the stone's energy cuts across space and time. Harnessing the power of the stone, he built a device called the W.I.S.P. It opens windows to any place and any time. Izzy now travels through time to see history unfold before her eyes. Although she must not change history, she can observe and investigate historical events.

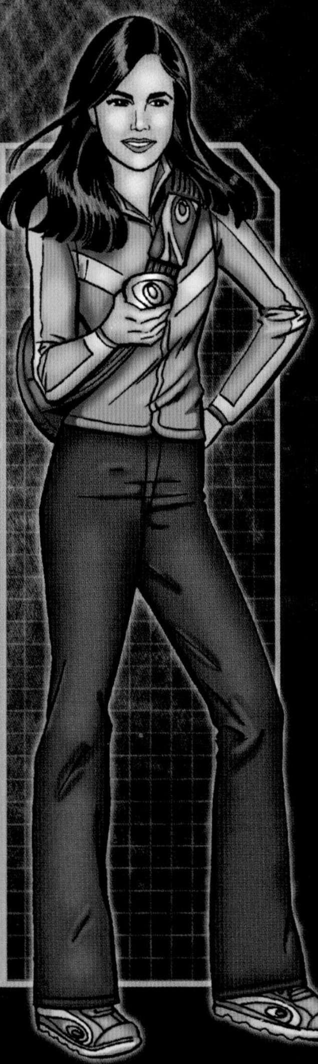

GLOSSARY

achievement (uh-CHEEV-muhnt) — a successful accomplishment, especially after a lot of effort

bamboo (bam-BOO) — a tropical grass with a hard, hollow stem

catapult (KAT-uh-puhlt) — a weapon used to hurl rocks, liquid, or other items at an enemy

crisis (KRYE-siss) — a time of danger or difficulty

dynasty (DYE-nuh-stee) — a series of rulers belonging to the same family or group

emperor (EM-pur-ur) — a male ruler of an empire; Chinese emperors made all the decisions for the people they ruled.

enthusiasm (en-THOO-zee-az-uhm) — great excitement or interest

myth (MITH) — a false idea that many people believe

peasant (PEZ-uhnt) — a poor person who owns a small farm or works on a farm, especially in Europe and some Asian countries

philosophy (fuh-LOSS-uh-fee) — the study of truth, wisdom, the nature of reality, and knowledge

primitive (PRIM-uh-tiv) — relating to an early stage of development

sorcery (SOR-sur-ee) — magic that controls evil spirits

stampede (stam-PEED) — when a group of animals makes a sudden, wild rush in one direction, usually because something has frightened them

READ MORE

Guillain, Charlotte. *Ancient China*. China Focus. Chicago: Heinemann Library, 2008.

Mah, Adeline Yen. *China: Land of Dragons and Emperors*. New York: Delacorte Press, 2009.

Morley, Jacqueline. *You Wouldn't Want to Work on the Great Wall of China!: Defenses You'd Rather Not Build*. New York: Franklin Watts, 2006.

O'Neill, Joseph R. *The Great Wall of China*. Essential Events. Edina, Minn.: ABDO, 2009.

Wilkinson, Philip. *Chinese Myth: A Treasury of Legends, Art, and History*. The World of Mythology. Armonk, N.Y.: Sharpe Focus, 2008.

INTERNET SITES

FactHound offers a safe, fun way to find Internet sites related to this book. All sites on FactHound have been researched by our staff.

Here's all you do:

Visit *www.facthound.com*

FactHound will fetch the best sites for you!

INDEX

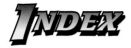